D1636967

LUST

A DICTIONARY FOR THE INSATIABLE

JENNIFER M. WOOD

Aadams media
Avon, Massachusetts

Published by
Adams Media, a division of F+W Media, Inc.
57 Littlefield Street, Avon, MA 02322. U.S.A.
www.adamsmedia.com

ISBN 10: 1-4405-2804-7
ISBN 13: 978-1-4405-2804-0
eISBN 10: 1-4405-2831-4
eISBN 13: 978-1-4405-2831-6

Printed in the United States of America.

10   9   8   7   6   5   4   3   2   1

Library of Congress Cataloging-in-Publication Data
is available from the publisher.

This publication is designed to provide accurate and authoritative information with regard to the subject matter covered. It is sold with the understanding that the publisher is not engaged in rendering legal, accounting, or other professional advice. If legal advice or other expert assistance is required, the services of a competent professional person should be sought.

—From a *Declaration of Principles* jointly adopted by a Committee of the American Bar Association and a Committee of Publishers and Associations

Many of the designations used by manufacturers and sellers to distinguish their product are claimed as trademarks. Where those designations appear in this book and Adams Media was aware of a trademark claim, the designations have been printed with initial capital letters.

Interior illustration © clipart.com

This book is available at quantity discounts for bulk purchases.
For information, please call 1-800-289-0963.

An Introduction to
Lust

lust

(luhst)

NOUN: Uncontrolled sexual desire.

The heat of lustful passion has singed the page since words first touched the sheets. From Ovid's multifarious lovers to Shakespeare's exhibition of desire in "Sonnet 129" to Lawrence's loss of inhibitions with Lady Chatterley and her lover, the stories of those in the throes of desire have intrigued and excited for ages. These arousing tales have allowed readers to live vicariously through the steamy trysts, naughty thoughts, and lecherous actions. The power of sexual temptation can tap into the physical desires innate in us all. While lust is defined best by that look in a lover's eye, this attractive dictionary does its best to capture the spirit of the most carnal sin.

A

ache
(*ayk*)
VERB: To long for; to feel pain.

admirer
(*ad-MYUHR-er*)
NOUN: One who has particular regard for someone or something.

Adonis
(*uh-DON-is*)
NOUN: From Greek mythology, an *Adonis* is an attractive young man.

adulation
(*AJ-uh-lay-shun*)
NOUN: Extreme praise or flattery, particularly that which seems obsequious or unmerited; worship.

> *Patrick's excessive ADULATION indicated to her that he wanted to be more than just friends.*

adult
(*uh-DUHLT*)
ADJECTIVE: Something that pertains to a grown-up; unsuitable for young people.

adulteress

(*uh-DUHL-ter-is*)

NOUN: A woman who commits adultery.

adulterine

(*uh-DUHL-tuh-reen*)

ADJECTIVE: Relating to an adulterous relationship.

adultery

(*uh-DUHL-tuh-ree*)

NOUN: A sexual relationship occurring between a married person and someone who is not his or her spouse.

affection

(*uh-FEK-shun*)

NOUN: Tenderness; fondness.

affinity

(*uh-FIN-ih-tee*)

NOUN: A natural fondness of affection.

afterglow

(*AF-ter-gloh*)

NOUN: A pleasurable feeling that follows a positive experience; afterlight.

agog
(*uh-GOG*)
ADJECTIVE: Unbridled excitement, eagerness, or desire.

alluring
(*uh-LOOR-ing*)
ADJECTIVE: Enticing; seductive.

amativeness
(*AM-uh-tiv-nes*)
NOUN: Feelings of love; amorousness.

amatory
(*AM-uh-tawr-ee*)
ADJECTIVE: Relating to the physical act of lovemaking.

amoral
(*ay-MAWR-uhl*)
ADJECTIVE: Having no moral standards, restraints, or principles.

amorous
(*AM-er-uhs*)
ADJECTIVE: Pertaining to love, particularly on a sexual level.

amour

(uh-MOOR)

NOUN: A secret love affair.

anaphrodisiac

(an-af-ruh-DEE-zee-ak)

NOUN: A substance that serves to decrease one's sexual desire; can also be used to describe something that acts as an anaphrodisiac.

anatomy

(uh-NAT-uh-mee)

NOUN: The human body.

androgynous

(an-DROJ-uh-nuhs)

ADJECTIVE: Having both male and female characteristics.

> *The main character's ANDROGYNOUS appearance resulted in more than one unconventionally alluring situation in the novel.*

animalism

(AN-uh muh-liz-uhm)

NOUN: The exhibition of behavior that is typical of animals in that one is guided by physical or carnal pleasures rather than emotional ones.

anorgasmic

(*an-awr-GAZ-mik*)

ADJECTIVE: Unable to achieve an orgasm during sex.

aphrodisia

(*af-ruh-DEE-zhuh*)

NOUN: Sexual desire.

> *A cold shower was an attempt to cull the overpowering*
> *APHRODISIA he was experiencing.*

aphrodisiac

(*af-ruh-DEE-ze-ak*)

NOUN: A substance that arouses sexual desire.

apolaustic

(*ap-oh-LAWS-tik*)

ADJECTIVE: Devoted to pleasure; hedonistic.

appealing

(*uh-PEE-ling*)

ADJECTIVE: Attractiveness; a quality or group of qualities that make something desirable to another.

appetence

(*AP-ih-tuhns*)

NOUN: Desire; appetite.

Promiscuity is like never

reading past the first page.

Monogamy is like reading

the same book over and over.

—MASON COOLEY

appetite

(*AP-ih-tyt*)

NOUN: A desire or craving for something, most often used in reference to food.

appetitive

(*AP-ih-ty-tiv*)

ADJECTIVE: Relating to appetite or craving.

ardent

(*AHR-dnt*)

ADJECTIVE: Enthusiastic or passionate; zealous.

ardor

(*AHR-der*)

NOUN: Intense desire or devotion; passion.

arouse

(*uh-ROWZ*)

VERB: To awaken; to sexually excite; to anger.

attachment

(*uh-TACH-muhnt*)

NOUN: Bond between people or things; affection.

attraction

(*uh-TRAK-shuhn*)

NOUN: A power that draws things together; magnetism.

B

bagnio

(*BAN-yoh*)

NOUN: A brothel.

bait

(*bayt*)

NOUN: Something used as a way to lure or attract somebody.

base

(*bays*)

ADJECTIVE: Immoral or dishonorable; low-quality.

bawd

(*bawd*)

NOUN: A prostitute or a madam who hires prostitutes.

bawdry

(*BAW-dree*)

NOUN: Obscene talk or language.

bawdy

(*BAW-dee*)

ADJECTIVE: Vulgar or lewd, though often meant in a humorous fashion.

beckon

(*BEK-uhn*)

VERB: To coax or entice.

bed

(*bed*)

VERB: As a noun, it is the place one sleeps; as a verb, it means to take a lover to that place.

> *In modern times, it is seemingly common practice for those in romantic relationships to BED before they wed.*

bedfellow

(*BED-fel-oh*)

NOUN: One who shares a bed.

bedmate

(*BED-meyt*)

NOUN: A spouse or lover.

beguile

(*bih-GYL*)

VERB: Entrance; deceive.

besotted

(*bih-SOT-ted*)

ADJECTIVE: To become foolish or confused, as a result of one's attraction to someone; smitten.

Lust is a mysterious wound

in the side of humanity; or

rather, at the very source

of its life! To confound this

lust in man with that desire

which unites the sexes is

like confusing a tumor

with the very organ which

it devours, a tumor whose

very deformity horribly

reproduces the shape.

—GEORGES BERNANOS

bewitch

(*bih-WICH*)

VERB: Enchant; cast a spell as in witchcraft.

billet-doux

(*BIL-ay-DOO*)

NOUN: A love letter.

bisexual

(*by-SEK-shoo-uhl*)

ADJECTIVE: Being sexually attracted to members of the same sex as well as the opposite sex.

bliss

(*blis*)

NOUN: A state of complete happiness; ecstasy.

A romantic tropical getaway was sheer BLISS for the newly married couple.

bodily

(*BOD-ih-lee*)

ADJECTIVE: Of or relating to the body; corporal.

bosomy

(*BOOZ-uh-mee*)

ADJECTIVE: A woman endowed with large breasts.

boudoir

(*BOO-dwahr*)

NOUN: A woman's bedroom or private sitting area; can be used as an adjective to describe something that might take place in a woman's bedroom.

breathless

(*BRETH-lis*)

ADJECTIVE: Having difficulty breathing because of physical exertion or a strong feeling, such as excitement; panting.

brothel

(*BROTH-uhl*)

NOUN: A whore house.

brutish

(*BROO-tish*)

ADJECTIVE: Carnal; cruel; coarse; uncivilized; animal-like.

buss

(*buhs*)

NOUN: A kiss.

> *Framed and hanging directly above the bed was the famous photograph of an uninhibited soldier firmly planting a BUSS on the lips of an unsuspecting female reveler.*

buxom

(*BUHK-suhm*)

ADJECTIVE: Curvaceous; used to describe a full-figured woman in particular.

C

cajole

(*kuh-JOHL*)

VERB: To convince someone to do something through flattery or sheer persistence.

callipygian

(*kal-uh-PIJ-ee-uhn*)

ADJECTIVE: Having a nicely shaped backside.

captivate

(*KAP-tuh-vayt*)

VERB: Entrance or enthrall.

> *To be a successful actor, one must possess an abundance of charisma and an unequivocal ability to both engage and CAPTIVATE an audience.*

caress

(*kuh-RESS*)

VERB: To touch in an affectionate manner; stroke.

carnal

(*KAHR-nuhl*)

ADJECTIVE: Relating to one's physical or sexual needs.

Casanova

(*kaz-uh-NOH-vuh*)

NOUN: A man who seduces women in quick succession; a playboy.

catch the eye

(*kach thuh aye*)

PHRASE: To stand out or grab the attention of.

charisma

(*kuh-RIZ-muh*)

NOUN: Likable personality trait that allows one to have a positive affect on others; magnetism or charm.

charm

(*chahrm*)

VERB: Captivate; using an attractive personality to convince someone to do something.

cicisbeo

(*chee-chiz-BEY-oh*)

NOUN: The lover of a married woman.

climactic

(*kly-MAK-tik*)
ADJECTIVE: Leading or pertaining to the culmination of something.

clinch

(*klinch*)
NOUN: An embrace or strong hold; clutch.

clitoral

(*KLIT-tohr-rawl*)
ADJECTIVE: Pertaining to the clitoris, a highly sensitive part of a female's genitalia.

coarse

(*kawrs*)
ADJECTIVE: Vulgar or uncouth; rough.

coax

(*kohks*)
VERB: To persuade in a gentle and kind manner; sweet-talk.

coitus

(*KOH-i-tuhs*)
NOUN: Sexual intercourse.

come-hither

(*kuhm-HITH-er*)

ADJECTIVE: Seductive; alluring.

come-on

(*KUHM-on*)

NOUN: A pickup line or other tactic one uses to try and seduce another.

comely

(*KUHM-lee*)

ADJECTIVE: Attractive or pleasant to look at; the word is most often used to describe a woman.

compulsion

(*kuhm-PUHL-shuhn*)

NOUN: An impulse; the act of forcing somebody to do something.

concubine

(*KONG-kyuh-byn*)

NOUN: Traditionally, it refers to the mistress of a married man who is looked after by her lover in the form of financial compensation and a home.

> *Rumors swirled around the office that the executive's secretary was actually his CONCUBINE, and her subsequent silence on the matter spoke volumes about her innocence.*

concupiscent

(*kon-KYOO-pi-suhnt*)

ADJECTIVE: Desirous, particularly of a sexual nature; lustful.

condom

(*KON-duhm*)

NOUN: A tight-fitting sheath, often made of latex, that a man fits over his penis during sex to prevent pregnancy or the spread of an STD.

conjugal

(*KON-juh-guhl*)

ADJECTIVE: Relating to marriage; connubial.

> *Approaching their tenth anniversary, the couple became interested in exploring ways to make CONJUGAL intimacy more exciting and spontaneous.*

consummate

(*KON-suh-mayt*)

VERB: To bring something to the point of completion or finality; to *consummate* a relationship or marriage, a couple enters into a sexual relationship.

copulate

(*KOP-yuh-layt*)

VERB: To engage in sexual activity.

Men decide far more problems by hate, love, lust, rage, sorrow, joy, hope, fear, illusion, or some other inward emotion than by reality, authority, any legal standard, judicial precedent, or statute.

—MARCUS TULLIUS CICERO

coquettish

(koh-KET-tish)

ADJECTIVE: Flirtatious; the word is almost always used in reference to a woman rather than a man.

corporeal

(kawr-PAWR-ee-uhl)

ADJECTIVE: Pertaining to or part of the body.

cougar

(KOO-ger)

NOUN: Slang term for an older woman who is only interested in younger men.

coupling

(KUHP-ling)

NOUN: To pair two things or people together as a couple; a sexual relationship.

court

(kawrt)

VERB: To expend time and energy trying to win someone over, often for romantic purposes; woo.

courtesan

(*KAWR-tuh-zuhn*)

NOUN: The mistress or regular prostitute of a wealthy man who is showered in gifts and status.

covet

(*KUHV-it*)

VERB: To want something that belongs to someone else.

crave

(*krayv*)

VERB: To have a strong desire for something; yearn.

Lonely and missing him desperately, the jilted lover felt an undeniable CRAVING to feel his skin against hers.

crude

(*krood*)

ADJECTIVE: Vulgar or obscene.

crush

(*kruhsh*)

NOUN: A fleeting romantic infatuation or the object of that infatuation.

cuddle

(*KUHD-l*)

VERB: To hold someone close in a comfortable, loving way; snuggle.

curvaceous

(*kur-VAY-shuhs*)

ADJECTIVE: Having a voluptuous shape.

cynosure

(*SY-nuh-shoor*)

NOUN: A person or thing that attracts a lot of attention or admiration; a directional guide.

D

dalliance

(*DAL-ee-uhns*)

NOUN: A brief flirtation or romantic affair that is not meant to be serious; dilly-dallying.

debauchery

(*dih-BAW-chuh-ree*)

NOUN: Excessively self-indulgent behavior, particularly those related to sexual pleasure; depravity.

deflower

(*dih-FLOW-er*)

VERB: To take one's virginity.

delight

(*dih-LYT*)

VERB: To take pleasure in something or to provide pleasure.

Delilah

(*dih-LY-luh*)

NOUN: A temptress; the word is Biblical in its origin, from the name of Samson's mistress, who took away his strength by cutting off his hair.

demimonde

(*DEM-ee-mond*)

NOUN: Originally used in reference to a prostitute or courtesan, this French word describes a class of people—especially women—with loose morals, particularly in regards to their sexual morals.

depravity

(*dih-PRAV-ih-tee*)

NOUN: Wickedness; moral corruption.

> *In the United States, prostitution is equated with moral DEPRAVITY and does not take into account the circumstances by which women are led to choose such a lifestyle.*

desiderate

(*dih-SID-uh-rayt*)

VERB: To think about or express a longing for something.

desideratum

(*dih-sid-uh-RAY-tuhm*)

NOUN: Something that is desired or needed.

desire

(*dih-ZY-uhr*)

NOUN: A longing or craving for something, and can specifically relate a longing for a sexual relationship with someone; sexual appetite.

desirous

(*dih-ZY-uhr-uhs*)

ADJECTIVE: Having desire for something.

deviant

(*DEE-vee-uhnt*)

NOUN: One whose behavior, particularly his or her sexual behavior, differs from what is considered normal or acceptable.

Dionysian

(*dy-uh-NISH-uhn*)

ADJECTIVE: Referencing Dionysius, the Greek god of revelry, *Dionysian* describes uninhibited or hedonistic behavior typically involving alcohol and promiscuity.

> *For a study on human sexuality and relationships, researchers headed to a local college campus to observe DIONYSIAN behavior first hand.*

dirty

(*DUR-tee*)

ADJECTIVE: Obscene or foul; something that is covered in dirt or filth; dishonest; unpleasant.

dirty-minded

(*DUR-tee-myn-did*)

ADJECTIVE: Having a mind full of vulgar thoughts.

dirty talk

(*DUR-tee tawk*)

NOUN: Erotic discussion that takes place during, as a prelude to, or in place of a sexual encounter.

discreet

(*dih-SKREET*)

ADJECTIVE: Showing tact in one's behavior; circumspect.

dishabille

(*dis-uh-BEEL*)

NOUN: From the French word meaning "to undress," *dishabille* refers to someone in a state of partial undress or whose appearance is very casual or careless.

I lost the love of heaven

above,

I spurned the lust of earth

below,

I felt the sweets of fancied

love,

And hell itself my only

foe.

—John Clare

dissolute

(*DIS-uh-loot*)

ADJECTIVE: Showing a lack of moral restraint when it comes to engaging in physical pleasures; debauched.

divest

(*dih-VEST*)

VERB: To take something away from someone; to remove something, including clothing.

divulge

(*dih-VUHLJ*)

VERB: To reveal information that was meant to be confidential; reveal.

dolce vita

(*DAWL-che VEE-tah*)

NOUN: Known as the "sweet life," it's a life full of self-indulgence and hedonistic pleasures.

dominatrix

(*dom-uh-NAY-triks*)

NOUN: A female who dominates a sadomasochistic relationship; the word can be used more broadly in reference to a woman who dominates a situation or relationship.

Don Juan

(*don WAHN*)

NOUN: A man who engages in a series of meaning-less flings with a series of women.

Exuding swagger and confidence, the young DON JUAN entered the bar alone but was determined to leave with one or more ladies on his arm.

dote

(*doht*)

VERB: Usually followed by "on" or "upon," to dote is to be extremely fond of a person or thing.

doxy

(*DOK-see*)

NOUN: The female in a sexual relationship; a pro-miscuous woman or prostitute.

E

eager

(*EE-ger*)

ADJECTIVE: Enthusiastic and looking forward to a thing or activity; excited.

easy

(*EE-zee*)

ADJECTIVE: Not difficult; *easy* is also used to describe a person with loose sexual morals.

> *Just because she was dressed provocatively for the occasion, Emma did not feel she deserved to be labeled as free and EASY.*

ebullition

(*eb-uh-LISH-uhn*)

NOUN: A sudden and powerful outburst of emotion; the act of bubbling up or boiling over, as in a liquid.

ecstatic

(*ek-STAT-ik*)

ADJECTIVE: Feeling great delight; blissful.

effusion

(*ih-FYOO-zhuhn*)

NOUN: An emotional outpouring of speech or writing.

emotion

(*ih-MOH-shuhn*)

NOUN: A feeling, including happiness, sadness, love, or hate.

enamor

(*ih-NAM-er*)

VERB: To captivate.

enchant

(*en-CHANT*)

VERB: To fascinate, captivate, or bewitch.

endear

(*en-DEER*)

VERB: To make a person or thing liked.

engross

(*en-GROHS*)

VERB: To consume one's attention; captivate.

enrapture

(*en-RAP-cher*)

VERB: To captivate or beguile.

enthrall

(*en-THRAWL*)

VERB: To thoroughly delight or captivate someone; rivet.

entice

(*en-TYS*)

VERB: To tempt or lure with something desirable.

entrance

(*en-TRAHNS*)

VERB: To captivate someone and hold his or her attention; enrapture.

entrap

(*en-TRAP*)

VERB: To tempt someone to do something wrong or immoral.

erogenous

(*ih-ROJ-uh-nuhs*)

ADJECTIVE: Something, like an area of the body, that is especially susceptible to sexual arousal.

Love wants to enjoy in other
ways the human being whom
it has enjoyed in bed; it looks
forward to having breakfast.
But in the morning Lust is
always furtive. It dresses as
mechanically as it undressed
and heads straight for the door,
to return to its own solitude.

—Henry Fairlie

eros

(*EER-os*)

NOUN: Derived from Eros, the Greek god of love, *eros* refers to sexual love or libido.

erotic

(*ih-ROT-ik*)

ADJECTIVE: Possessing the ability to arouse sexual desire in someone.

eroticize

(*ih-ROT-uh-syz*)

VERB: To sexualize something.

erotism

(*AYR-uh-tiz-uhm*)

NOUN: An erotic quality; feelings of sexual arousal; also known as *eroticism*.

One of the oldest and most notable books on sex and EROTICISM is the Kama Sutra, which was probably written in the first century.

euphoria

(*yoo-FAWR-ee-uh*)

NOUN: A state of extreme happiness or well-being; ecstasy.

exhibitionism

(*ek-suh-BISH-uh-niz-uhm*)

NOUN: The desire to attract attention from loud, aggressive behavior; a psychological compulsion to expose oneself in public.

explicit

(*ik-SPLIS-it*)

ADJECTIVE: Extremely detailed so as to leave no room for interpretation; sexually graphic.

F

fancy

(*FAN-see*)

VERB: To be attracted to someone in a romantic or sexual way; to believe in—but not be 100 percent certain of—something; to imagine.

fantasize

(*FAN-tuh-syz*)

VERB: To concoct romantic or extravagant notions in one's head; daydream.

fascination

(*fas-uh-NAY-shuhn*)

NOUN: To be completely mesmerized by a person or thing; captivation.

femme fatale

(*fem fuh-TAL*)

NOUN: A devious woman who uses her attractiveness and sex appeal to lure men into doing her dirty work, which often includes murder. The stereotype was made famous in the movies in the 1940s.

fervor

(*FUR-ver*)

NOUN: Extreme passion or dedication; ardor.

fetish

(*FET-ish*)

NOUN: A thing—usually something other than an erogenous body part—that is worshipped in a sexual fashion; any object, activity, or idea with which one develops a fixation.

fidelity

(*fi-DEL-ih-tee*)

NOUN: Faithfulness or loyalty; accuracy.

filthiness

(*FIL-thee*)

ADJECTIVE: Extremely dirty or foul; vulgar or obscene.

> *Many people are turned off by sadomasochism as a sexual practice and see it as the epitome of FILTHINESS and immorality.*

fixate

(*FIK-sayt*)

VERB: To become completely consumed or obsessed by something.

flagitious

(*fluh-JISH-uhs*)

ADJECTIVE: Shamefully scandalous; disgraceful.

flagrant

(*FLAY-gruhnt*)

ADJECTIVE: Glaringly obvious; scandalous.

Stella's FLAGRANT flaunting of her womanly assets put a bad taste in the mouths of the other members of the committee.

flame

(*flaym*)

NOUN: A person for whom one carries a torch; an object of desire; extreme passion; burning gas or vapor.

flaunt

(*flawnt*)

VERB: To accentuate one's positive attributes, be it a shapely body or great wealth.

fleshly

(*FLESH-lee*)

ADJECTIVE: Relating to the flesh or human body; sensual.

fling

(*fling*)

NOUN: A short-lived sexual dalliance.

flirtation

(*flur-TAY-shuhn*)

NOUN: Behaving in a coquettish or playfully seductive way; a brief but not serious romantic dalliance.

fondle

(*FON-dl*)

VERB: To stroke or touch someone in an affectionate manner; caress.

fondness

(*FOND-nis*)

NOUN: Affection or liking.

foreplay

(*FAWR-play*)

NOUN: A period of sexual stimulation leading up to sexual intercourse.

fornication

(*fawr-ni-KAY-shuhn*)

NOUN: Consensual sex between two people; as referenced in the Bible, it is used in a negative fashion to connote an immoral sexual relationship between two unmarried persons.

fornicatress

(*fawr-ni-KAY-tress*)

NOUN: A woman engaged in adultery.

forwardness

(*FAWR-werd-nis*)

NOUN: Behavior that is bold or presumptuous in relation to normal levels of modesty.

foul

(*fowl*)

ADJECTIVE: Impure or obscene; dirty; offending the senses.

foxy

(*FOK-see*)

ADJECTIVE: Attractive; sexy.

freaky

(*FREE-kee*)

ADJECTIVE: Unconventional or strange; deviant.

free-living

(*FREE-LIV-ing*)

ADJECTIVE: Living life in a way where one feels free to follow his or her desires without guilt or moral reprobation.

But virtue, as it never

will be moved,

Though lewdness court it in a

shape of heaven,

So lust, though to a radiant

angel linked,

Will sate itself in a celestial bed

And prey on garbage

—WILLIAM SHAKESPEARE

frenzy

(*FREN-zee*)

NOUN: A state of wild excitement, anger, or other emotion.

In a FRENZY of passion and excitement, the two lovers ripped each others clothes off and raced to the bedroom.

frottage

(*fraw-TAHZH*)

NOUN: The act of rubbing against an object or person—often a stranger in a crowd—in order to attain sexual satisfaction; also called frotteurism.

G

gallant

(*GAL-uhnt*)

ADJECTIVE: Respectful, especially toward women; chivalrous.

genital

(*JEN-ih-ti*)

ADJECTIVE: Pertaining to one's sexual organs; relating to reproduction.

gigolo

(*JIG-uh-loh*)

NOUN: A male escort or prostitute.

goatish

(*GOH-tish*)

ADJECTIVE: Lustful; lewd.

graphic

(*GRAF-ik*)

ADJECTIVE: Explicit; extremely suggestive.

> *Due to the GRAPHIC sexual scenes in the movie, the audience was advised to watch at their own discretion.*

I can imagine myself on my

death-bed, spent utterly with

lust to touch the next world,

like a boy asking for his first

kiss from a woman.

—ALEISTER CROWLEY

gratification

(*grat-uh-fi-KAY-shuhn*)

NOUN: Satisfaction; a thing or action that gives one satisfaction.

gratuitous

(*gruh-TOO-ih-tuhs*)

ADJECTIVE: Uncalled for; lacking good reason.

gravitate

(*GRAV-ih-tayt*)

VERB: To have a natural inclination or attraction to a thing or person.

gynecomania

(*gy-ni-KO-may-nee-uh*)

NOUN: An overpowering enthusiasm for women.

H

hanker

(*hang-ker*)

VERB: To crave or want something desperately; yearn.

hanky-panky

(*HANG-kee-PANG-kee*)

NOUN: Sexual activity; fooling around.

As Jake opened the door to the conference room he was shocked to see two of his coworkers engaging in HANKY-PANKY.

hardcore

(*HAHRD-KAWR*)

ADJECTIVE: Depicting sex or sexual situations in a graphic manner; extremely dedicated.

harlot

(*HAHR-luht*)

NOUN: A prostitute or promiscuous woman.

heartbreaker

(*HAHRT-bray-ker*)

NOUN: A person with whom many people fall in love but who often hurts those people in the end.

hedonist
(*HEED-n-ist*)
NOUN: One whose entire life is dedicated to the pursuit or pleasure.

hentai
(*hen-tay*)
NOUN: A sexually explicit graphic novel or comic.

horny
(*HAWR-nee*)
ADJECTIVE: Sexually aroused or lustful; having horns.

hot-blooded
(*HOT-BLUHD-id*)
ADJECTIVE: Passionate; adventuresome.

hot pants
(*hot pants*)
NOUN: Very strong sexual desire; very short and tight-fitting shorts that became popular with women in the 1970s.

the hots
(*thuh hotz*)
NOUN: Attraction; sexual desire.

When I heard the Earth-song,

I was no longer brave;

My avarice cooled

Like lust in the

chill of the grave

—Ralph Waldo Emerson

hunger

(*HUHNG-ger*)

NOUN: A strong desire or need; the word is most often used in reference to food.

hunky

(*HUHNG-kee*)

ADJECTIVE: A handsome, sexy man.

hussy

(*HUHS-ee*)

NOUN: An immoral or poorly behaved woman; trollop.

> *After only three weeks, Janet had already acquired a reputation as a brazen HUSSY by all the housewives in the upper-class neighborhood.*

I

immodest

(*ih-MOD-ist*)

ADJECTIVE: Not showing modesty in one's behavior; shameless.

immoral

(*ih-MAWR-uhl*)

NOUN: A manner that goes against socially accepted morals; depravity.

> *Former U.S. president Bill Clinton was impeached as a direct result of his promiscuous and IMMORAL actions while in the White House.*

impassioned

(*im-PASH-uhnd*)

ADJECTIVE: Full of intense emotions; fervent.

impotence

(*IM-puh-tuhns*)

NOUN: A male's inability to perform or complete sexual intercourse; more generally, impotence refers to weakness.

improbity

(*im-PROH-bi-tee*)

NOUN: Dishonesty or lack of a moral conscience.

improper

(*im-PROP-er*)

ADJECTIVE: Inappropriate or incorrect; the term is most often used to describe one's behavior or manners.

impropriety

(*im-pruh-PRY-ih-tee*)

NOUN: Inappropriate behavior; indecency.

impudicity

(*im-pyoo-DIS-ih-tee*)

NOUN: Lacking modesty or shame; immodesty.

impure

(*im-PYOOR*)

ADJECTIVE: Contaminated with sin; polluted with a harmful or inferior substance.

in flagrante delicto

(*in fluh-GRAN-tee di-LIK-toh*)

PHRASE: In the act or in the midst of sexual activity.

inamorata

(*in-am-uh-RAH-tuh*)

NOUN: A female object of love and desire.

incite
(*in-SYT*)
VERB: To stir up emotion or stimulate action;
provoke.

inclination
(*in-kluh-NAY-shuhn*)
NOUN: A particular disposition or preference;
proclivity.

incontinence
(*in-KON-tn-uhns*)
NOUN: The inability to control one's sexual appetite.

indecent
(*in-DEE-suhnt*)
ADJECTIVE: Inappropriate or unseemly; offensive.

indelicate
(*in-DEL-ih-kit*)
ADJECTIVE: Lacking delicacy of language; tactless
or crude.

indiscreet
(*in-di-SKREET*)
ADJECTIVE: Lacking discretion or good judgment;
imprudent.

indiscriminate

(*in-di-SKRIM-uh-nit*)

ADJECTIVE: Showing carelessness in one's choices; arbitrary or haphazard.

indulgent

(*in-DUHL-juhnt*)

ADJECTIVE: Being generous with the granting of someone's wishes or desires, including your own.

infatuation

(*in-fach-oo-AY-shuhn*)

NOUN: An extreme—but often fleeting—obsession with a person, thing, or activity; *infatuation* is also used in reference to the person or thing with which one is obsessed.

> *The innocent schoolgirl quickly became INFATUATED with the brilliant and attractive new professor.*

infidelity

(*in-fi-DEL-ih-tee*)

NOUN: Unfaithfulness or disloyalty to one's significant other; to be less than in quality.

The oftener seen,

the more I lust.

—Barnabe Googe

inflame

(*in-FLAYM*)

VERB: To arouse an intense emotion, such as jealousy, in someone; to further ignite an emotion that already exists.

iniquitous

(*ih-NIK-wi-tuhs*)

ADJECTIVE: Sinful or immoral; wicked.

innuendo

(*in-yoo-EN-doh*)

NOUN: A subtle hint or suggestion by way of a seemingly innocuous remark; an insinuation.

insatiable

(*in-SAY-shuh-buhl*)

ADJECTIVE: Incapable of being satisfied or appeased; unquenchable.

In that moment, the INSATIABLE thirst of the vampire was fully realized, and his victim's blood-curdling scream could be heard for miles around.

inseparable

(*in-SEP-er-uh-buhl*)

ADJECTIVE: Unable to be separated.

insinuate

(*in-SIN-yoo-yet*)

VERB: To hint at or imply something negative; to slowly ingratiate oneself.

intemperance

(*in-TEM-per-uhns*)

NOUN: A lack of self-restraint; the satisfaction of a hedonistic desire.

intercourse

(*IN-ter-kawrs*)

NOUN: An exchange between two or more people; sexual *intercourse* refers to the act of lovemaking.

intimacy

(*IN-tuh-muh-see*)

NOUN: The closeness that exists between two people in a personal relationship; in a less formal way, can be used in reference to a sexual relationship.

inveigle

(*in-VAY-guhl*)

VERB: To convince someone to act in a way not typical to his or her behavior through charm or flattery; beguile.

itch

(*ich*)

NOUN: A desire for something; a sensation that forces one to scratch.

ithyphallic

(*ith-uh-FAL-ik*)

ADJECTIVE: The depiction of an erect penis in a piece of art.

> *Reportedly, the museum refused to allow the ITHYPHALLIC work to be displayed in the main gallery out of fear that it was not appropriate for all viewers.*

J and K

Jezebel

(*JEZ-uh-bel*)

NOUN: A wicked, scheming woman; the wicked Tyrean princess who married King Ahab in the Bible.

John

(*jon*)

NOUN: A man who solicits a prostitute.

jump (someone's) bones

(*juhmp SUHM-wuhnz bohnz*)

VERB: To engage in sexual intercourse with a person.

Kama Sutra

(*KOM-uh SOO-truh*)

NOUN: An ancient Sanskrit text that provides information on sexual behavior and techniques.

kink

(*kingk*)

NOUN: An odd interest or proclivity, especially in relation to sexual desires; a twist or tangle in something that is otherwise straight, like a rope or hose.

kinky

(*KING-kee*)

ADJECTIVE: Possessing unconventional or peculiar sexual tastes.

Henry thought he was sexually adventurous; however, after rendezvousing with Cynthia and getting a taste of her KINKY preferences, he realized he's a little more vanilla than he thought.

Kinsey scale

(*KIN-zee skayl*)

NOUN: A scale developed by American biologist Alfred Kinsey that rates a person's sexuality from zero (exclusively heterosexual) to six (exclusively homosexual), with one to five indicating bisexuality.

kiss

(*kis*)

VERB: To press one's lips against another's, usually in a show of affection.

L

ladies' man

(*LAY-deez man*)

NOUN: A man who dates a lot of women.

ladykiller

(*LAY-dee-kil-er*)

NOUN: A man who women find irresistible; a ladies' man.

ladylove

(*LAY-dee-luhv*)

NOUN: A woman with whom a man is involved and in love.

lascivious

(*luh-SIV-see-uhs*)

ADJECTIVE: Lustful or lewd; displaying an inappropriate interest in sex.

laxity

(*LAK-si-tee*)

NOUN: Not being strict or careful; careless.

lead on

(*leed on*)

VERB: To mislead or deceive someone.

lecher

(*LECH-er*)

NOUN: A man who behaves in an inappropriately lustful or salacious manner.

lewd

(*lood*)

ADJECTIVE: Obscene or indecent.

liaison

(*lee-ay-ZAWN*)

NOUN: An illicit sexual relationship.

The couple's sexual LIAISON is as risky as it is steamy, as they must plan behind their married partners' backs in order to meet for their trysts.

libertine

(*LIB-er-teen*)

NOUN: Most often used in reference to a man, a *libertine* is one who engages in immorality and promiscuity.

libido

(*li-BEE-doh*)

NOUN: Sex drive.

licentious

(*ly-SEN-shuhs*)

ADJECTIVE: Showing no restraint in the pursuit of pleasure—particularly that of a sexual nature—with no regard to morals; shameless.

liking

(*LY-king*)

NOUN: A fondness or tendency toward a particular thing or person; a feeling of pleasantness.

Lauren has taken a serious LIKING to her husband's revived sex drive; the two can hardly keep their hands off each other.

liquorish

(*LIK-er-ish*)

ADJECTIVE: Constantly thinking about or trying to pursue sexual relationships.

Lolita

(*loh-LEE-tuh*)

NOUN: From the Vladimir Nabokov novel of the same name, a *Lolita* is a young girl who attracts sexual desire from older men.

I have known a number of Don Juans who were good studs and who cavorted between the sheets without a psychiatrist to guide them. But most of the busy love-makers I knew were looking for masculinity rather than practicing it. They were fellows of dubious lust.

—Ben Hecht

longing

(*LAWNG-ing*)

NOUN: A strong desire for a person or thing; yearning.

loose

(*loos*)

ADJECTIVE: In a more general sense, it describes something that does not fit tightly; in reference to sexual relationships, it describes someone who is promiscuous or has many sexual partners, often choosing them indiscriminately.

Lothario

(*loh-THAYR-ee-oh*)

NOUN: A man who is constantly trying to seduce women.

lovemaking

(*LUHV-may-king*)

NOUN: Sexual intercourse.

> *Sex is no longer just sex for the pair as their emotional involvement heightens the intimacy and turns it into LOVEMAKING.*

lover

(*LUHV-er*)

NOUN: One who engages in sexual intercourse with another.

loverlike

(*LUHV-er*)

ADJECTIVE: Behavior that would be in the manner of a lover.

lubricant

(*LOO-bri-kuhnt*)

NOUN: A substance or material that helps to reduce friction between two moving parts.

lubricous

(*LOO-bri-kuhs*)

ADJECTIVE: Salacious or sexually exciting; slippery, as if something has been lubricated.

luscious

(*LUHSH-uhs*)

ADJECTIVE: Sexually and physically appealing; pleasingly rich or delicious.

lure

(*loor*)

VERB: To tempt or entice someone to go somewhere or do something with the promise of a pleasurable reward.

lustful

(*LUHST-fuhl*)

ADJECTIVE: Full of feelings of sexual desire; licentious.

> *With a LUSTFUL passion, the young woman entered into a long embrace with her separated lover as soon as he stepped off of the train.*

luxuria

(*LUHK-shuh-ree-ah*)

NOUN: Another word for lust, *luxuria* is an unrestrained sexual desire.

M

magnetism

(*MAG-ni-tiz-uhm*)

NOUN: A strong attractiveness in someone that draws others to him or her.

masturbate

(*MAS-ter-bayt*)

VERB: To find sexual gratification without a partner through the stimulation of one's own genitalia.

mate

(*mayt*)

VERB: To engage in sexual relations, typically with the purpose of procreation. As a noun, a *mate* can refer to one's lover or significant other.

ménage à trois

(*may-NAHZH ah trwah*)

NOUN: A sexual interlude between three people.

> *Not one to temper his sinful urges, the playboy decided he would not choose between the two women, but, instead, the three would have a MÉNAGE À TROIS.*

minx

(*mingks*)

NOUN: A flirtatious or promiscuous woman.

The human spirit sublimates

the impulses it thwarts:

a healthy sex life mitigates

the lust for other sports.

—PIET HEIN

mistress

(*MIS-tris*)

NOUN: The female lover of a man who is not his wife; the term *mistress* often implies that the extra-marital affair is a long-term or ongoing one.

monogamy

(*muh-NOG-uh-mee*)

NOUN: The commitment to either marry or date just one person at a time.

> *Just because one subscribes to the single-partner restrictions of MONOGAMY does not mean all lustful desires have to be squelched—it just means they are focused on one person in particular.*

multiorgasmic

(*MUHL-tee-AWR-gaz-mik*)

ADJECTIVE: Feeling more than one orgasm—usually one right after the other—in a single sexual encounter.

N

naked

(*NAY-kid*)

ADJECTIVE: To be without clothes; nude.

naughty

(*NAW-tee*)

ADJECTIVE: Playfully misbehaved; sinful.

necking

(*NEK-ing*)

NOUN: To kiss or caress in an amorous manner while fully clothed.

negligee

(*neg-li-ZHAY*)

NOUN: A woman's dressing gown, usually worn loose and made from a soft or sheer fabric.

nestle

(*NES-uhl*)

VERB: To position oneself in a comfortable position as close to another's body as possible.

Lying in bed after spending the afternoon reveling in carnal pleasure, Katherine NESTLED against her partner for a postcoital sleep.

Sodom and Madonna-ism

are two halves of the same

movement, the mere tick-

tack of lust and ascetism,

piety and pornography.

—D. H. LAWRENCE

nibble

(*NIB-uhl*)
VERB: To bite gently or playfully.

nipple

(*NIP-uhl*)
NOUN: A small projection near the center of the breast; considered an erogenous zone.

nocturnal emission

(*nok-TUR-nl ih-MISH-uhn*)
NOUN: Involuntary ejaculation during sleep, usually the result of an erotic dream.

nookie

(*NOOK-ee*)
NOUN: Slang word for sexual intercourse.

nooner

(*NOO-ner*)
NOUN: An often impromptu sexual dalliance that occurs in the middle of the day.

nubile

(*NOO-byl*)
ADJECTIVE: Sexually attractive and mature.

nude

(*nood*)

ADJECTIVE OR NOUN: As an adjective, unclothed. As a noun, a statue or painting of a naked human.

nuptial

(*NUHP-shul*)

ADJECTIVE: Pertaining to marriage or one's marital vows; matrimonial.

nuzzle

(*NUHZ-uhl*)

VERB: To show affection by rubbing one's nose in a playful manner on another person or thing.

nymph

(*nimf*)

NOUN: A beautiful young woman.

nymphet

(*nim-FET*)

NOUN: A young girl—typically in her early teens—who exudes sexual desire and, as such, attracts it from men.

nymphomaniac

(*nim-fuh-MAY-nee-ak*)

NOUN: A woman possessing an excessively uncontrollable desire for sex.

> *Cassandra proved herself to be a true NYPHOMANIAC, choosing to spend the entire vacation away in the bedroom with her lover.*

O

obscene

(*uhb-SEEN*)

ADJECTIVE: Lewd and offensive; not suitable for public consumption because of its disregard for basic humanity or morals.

> *Unable to contain their lustful passion, the couple chose to do the OBSCENE and make love right there in the park's woods, visible to anyone who happened to walk by.*

obscenity

(*uhb-SEN-i-tee*)

NOUN: Something—including a word or phrase— that is morally reprehensible.

obsession

(*uhb-SESH-uhn*)

NOUN: A fascination with a person, thing, or idea that fully occupies one's mind; fixation.

off-color

(*awf-KUHL-er*)

ADJECTIVE: Uncouth, particularly in relation to something that is sexually suggestive.

ogle

(*OH-guhl*)

VERB: To eyeball someone in a flirtatious way in order to convey one's attraction.

I know love and lust

don't always keep

the same company.

—Stephenie Meyer

one-night stand

(*WUHN-nyt stand*)

NOUN: A one-time sexual engagement with someone.

orgasm

(*AWR-gaz-uhm*)

NOUN: The physical and emotional climax experienced at the peak of sexual excitement; the word can also be used as a verb to describe the process of experiencing an orgasm.

orgiastic

(*awr-jee-AS-tik*)

ADJECTIVE: Marked by debauchery or licentiousness; in the spirit of an orgy.

orgy

(*AWR-jee*)

NOUN: A wild gathering characterized by unrestrained, hedonistic behavior, including promiscuous sex and excessive drinking.

Between the sexual energy in the air and the bottles of wine being finished, it was only a matter of time before the clothes started coming off and the intimate get-together turned into a wild ORGY.

osculate

(*OS-kyuh-layt*)

VERB: To come together; to kiss.

oversexed

(*OH-ver-SEKST*)

ADJECTIVE: Demonstrating a preoccupation with sex.

P

paramour

(*PAR-uh-moor*)

NOUN: A lover, particularly one involved in an adulterous relationship.

paraphilia

(*par-uh-FIL-ee-uh*)

NOUN: A predilection for deviant sexual practices, such as sadomasochism or fetishism.

pareunia

(*pah-roo-NEE-ah*)

NOUN: Sexual intercourse.

passion

(*PASH-uhn*)

NOUN: An overwhelming emotion, such as love or hatred; intense sexual desire; the object of one's interest.

The PASSION Richard possessed for Scarlet could not be contained and became palpable as the two moved from the table where they enjoyed dinner upstairs to his bed.

peccable

(*PEK-uh-buhl*)

ADJECTIVE: Having a tendency to fall prey to temptation; sinful.

Peeping Tom
(*PEE-ping tom*)
NOUN: A voyeur.

penchant
(*PEN-chuhnt*)
NOUN: A strong fondness or liking for something.

perversion
(*per-VUR-zhuhn*)
NOUN: A sexual practice or proclivity that is considered deviant.

petting
(*PET-ing*)
VERB: To fondle or caress in an effort to attain sexual satisfaction but without intercourse.

phallic
(*FAL-ik*)
ADJECTIVE: Resembling a penis.

philanderer
(*fi-LAN-der-er*)
NOUN: A man who cheats on his significant other.

Good gossip is just what's

going on. Bad gossip is stuff

that is salacious, mean,

and bitchy—the kind most

people really enjoy.

pine

(*pyn*)

VERB: To long for or yearn, particularly for something that is out of one's reach; languish.

As days turned into weeks, the two young lovers PINED for one another, and their longing could not be tempered by the handwritten love letters they sent each day.

pique

(*peek*)

VERB: To arouse one's interest or curiosity in something.

playboy

(*PLAY-boy*)

NOUN: A man who plays the field and dates many women at one time.

player

(*PLAY-er*)

NOUN: A man or woman who engages in a series of brief romantic relationships, often dating several people at the same time.

pleasure

(*PLEZH-er*)

NOUN: A feeling of enjoyment or satisfaction; sexual gratification.

polyamory

(*POL-ee-AY-muh-ree*)

NOUN: Engagement in multiple sexual relationships at one time.

polygamous

(*puh-LIG-uh-muhs*)

ADJECTIVE: Having more than one wife at the same time.

polymorphous perverse

(*pol-ee-MAWR-fuhs per-VURS*)

ADJECTIVE: Exhibiting immature sexual tendencies where one's genitals are not the source of erotic stimulation.

pornography

(*pawr-NOG-ruh-fee*)

NOUN: Sexually explicit materials in the form of movies, magazines, photos, and more.

postcoital

(*post-KOH-ih-tuhl*)

ADJECTIVE: Occurring after sexual intercourse.

While Anne enjoys every second of ecstasy that comes with sex, what really drives her wild are the POSTCOITAL moments right after climax when she's in her partner's arms.

predilection

(*pred-ih-LEK-shuhn*)

NOUN: An penchant or preference for something; inclination.

priapism

(*PRY-uh-piz-uhm*)

NOUN: A medical condition in which the penis remains erect but in the absence of sexual arousal.

private parts

(*PRY-vit pahrts*)

NOUN: One's external genital organs.

proclivity

(*proh-KLIV-ih-tee*)

NOUN: An inclination or tendency.

procreate

(*PROH-kree-ayt*)

VERB: Sexual relations for the purpose of reproduction.

promiscuous

(*pruh-MIS-kyoo-uhs*)

ADJECTIVE: Engaged in a series of indiscriminate sexual relationships.

prophylactic

(*proh-fuh-LAK-tik*)

NOUN: A condom or other device meant to prevent disease or conception during sex.

prostitution

(*pros-ti-TOO-shuhn*)

NOUN: The act of exchanging sexual acts for money or other financial gain.

provoke

(*pruh-VOHK*)

VERB: To incite or induce one to action; instigate.

prurient

(*PROOR-ee-uhnt*)

ADJECTIVE: Characterized by unwholesome or lustful thoughts.

pudendum

(*pyoo-DEN-duhm*)

NOUN: External genital organs, particularly those of the female.

pulchritudinous

(*puhl-kri-TOOD-n-uhs*)

ADJECTIVE: Physically beautiful; comely.

Q and R

quickie

(*KWIK-ee*)

NOUN: An activity that is performed in a hurry, especially a sexual act that is completed without pretense or foreplay.

> *In the first few weeks of their courtship, it was impossible for the couple to keep their hands off one another—and they would often visit each other's workplace to steal away for a QUICKIE.*

racy

(*RAY-see*)

ADJECTIVE: Slightly sexual or risqué.

rake

(*rayk*)

NOUN: A licentious man; womanizer.

randy

(*RAN-dee*)

ADJECTIVE: Sexually aroused; lustful.

rapture

(*RAP-cher*)

NOUN: A state of euphoria or bliss; ecstasy.

Only a struggle twists

sentimentality and lust

together into love.

—E. M. Forster

raunchy

(*RAWN-chee*)

ADJECTIVE: Obscene or bawdy; vulgar.

ravenous

(*RAV-uh-nuhs*)

ADJECTIVE: Extremely hungry or greedy; voracious.

ravish

(*RAV-ish*)

VERB: To present someone with an overwhelming burst of passion or emotion; to force or coerce someone into having sexual relations (the phrase can be used in consensual relationships to indicate the man is the one instigating).

rekindle

(*ree-KIN-dl*)

VERB: To reignite; to light afire something that has burned out.

relish

(*REL-ish*)

VERB: To enjoy or savor something that brings one pleasure.

revelry

(*REV-uhl-ree*)

NOUN: A noisy celebration that often includes excessive eating, drinking, and frivolity.

> *The newlywed's bedroom REVELRY could be heard loud and clear through the open balcony door.*

ribald

(*RIB-uhld*)

ADJECTIVE: Behaving in a vulgar or coarse manner, but often meant in a humorous way.

risqué

(*ri-SKAY*)

ADJECTIVE: Indecent or racy.

roué

(*roo-AY*)

NOUN: A man who leads a life of debauchery, filled with drinking, gambling, and women.

ruttish

(*RUHT-ish*)

ADJECTIVE: Lascivious or salacious.

S

sadism

(*SAY-diz-uhm*)
NOUN: Attaining sexual satisfaction by inflicting pain on one's partner; cruelty.

salacious

(*suh-LAY-shuhs*)
ADJECTIVE: Prone to incite sexual arousal or titillation; possessing lewd sexual interests.

saturnalia

(*sat-er-NAY-lee-uh*)
NOUN: A rowdy party or orgy.

satyriasis

(*sey-tuh-RY-uh-sis*)
NOUN: Uncontrollable male compulsion to have sex with as many individuals as possible.

saucy

(*SAW-see*)
ADJECTIVE: Brazen or forward, though often meant in a humorous manner.

scabrous

(SKAB-ruhs)

ADJECTIVE: Referring to sex in an obscene or risqué fashion; scandalous.

scandalous

(SKAN-dl-uhs)

ADJECTIVE: Shameful or improper; shocking.

seduction

(si-DUHK-shuhn)

NOUN: Persuasive behaviors—be they romantic or deceptive—that lead one person to have sex with another or be tempted in some other way.

> *Samantha's game of playing hard to get is part of her SEDUCTION; choosing to play it cool only makes her partners want her more and the sex that much hotter.*

self-gratification

(SELF-grat-uh-fi-KEY-shuhn)

NOUN: The act of satisfying one's own desires, particularly as it relates to sexual desires.

sensualist

(SEN-shoo-uh-list)

NOUN: One who lives his or her life in pursuit of luxury and pleasure.

sex drive

(*seks dryv*)

NOUN: One's individual level of need for sexual interactions; libido.

sex play

(*seks play*)

NOUN: Touching of an erotic nature that typical precedes intercourse; foreplay.

sexpert

(*seks-spurt*)

NOUN: An expert in matters related to sex, sometimes self-described.

sexual urge

(*SEK-shoo-uhl urj*)

NOUN: An overwhelming carnal desire or preference.

sexy

(*SEK-see*)

ADJECTIVE: A somewhat indefinable quality that makes an object or person sexually desirous to another.

shack up

(*shak uhp*)

VERB: To live together without being married; cohabitate.

shameless

(*SHAYM-lis*)

ADJECTIVE: Feeling a lack of embarrassment or humiliation in a situation where societal norms would call for it; unashamed.

shapely

(*SHAYP-lee*)

ADJECTIVE: An attractive bodily shape that inspires desire in others.

The lounge singer's SHAPELY silhouette grabbed the audience's attention as she began performing behind the stage's thin curtain.

sinful

(*SIN-fuhl*)

ADJECTIVE: Something that is characterized by unethical or contemptible behavior; wicked.

siren

(*SY-ruhn*)

NOUN: From Greek mythology, a *siren* is a beautiful young woman who tempts men with her seductive ways.

skirt chaser

(*skurt CHAY-ser*)

NOUN: A man in constant pursuit of women; womanizer.

slattern

(*SLAT-ern*)

NOUN: A promiscuous woman; slut.

sleep around

(*sleep uh-ROUND*)

VERB: Engaging in a promiscuous lifestyle.

> *He understood the reputation he was receiving due to all his SLEEPING AROUND, but the young man could not help himself from hopping into a different bed almost every day of the week.*

slut

(*sluht*)

NOUN: A derogatory term for a promiscuous person, most often a woman.

The lust for comfort, that

stealthy thing that enters the

house a guest,

and then becomes a host,

and then a master.

—Kahlil Gibran

smooch
(*smooch*)
VERB: To kiss.

smutty
(*SMUHT-ee*)
ADJECTIVE: Indecent or pornographic.

snuggle
(*SNUHG-uhl*)
VERB: To cuddle with another person in a comfortable manner; nestle.

softcore
(*SAWFT-KAWR*)
ADJECTIVE: Sexually arousing material that is not explicit.

spicy
(*SPY-see*)
ADJECTIVE: Somewhat risqué or scandalous.

spoon
(*spoon*)
VERB: To cuddle or nestle with another person very closely.

statuesque

(*stach-oo-ESK*)

ADJECTIVE: Possessing classic beauty, like a statue.

steamy

(*STEE-mee*)

ADJECTIVE: Excessively sexual or lusty; extreme heat or humidity.

stimulate

(*STIM-yuh-layt*)

VERB: To incite interest or arousal in a person or thing by means both mental and physical.

stripper

(*STRIP-er*)

NOUN: A person—usually a woman—who disrobes in front of others as a source of entertainment and is paid for it.

striptease

(*STRIP-teez*)

NOUN: A seductive act or dance in which a stripper or other performer undresses slowly in order to titillate his or her audience.

strumpet

(*STRUHM-pit*)

NOUN: A prostitute; harlot.

stud

(*stuhd*)

NOUN: A man well-versed in the ways of sexual relations and often deemed a great lover.

submissive

(*suhb-MIS-iv*)

ADJECTIVE: Obedience without protest; compliant.

sugar daddy

(*SHOOG-er DAD-ee*)

NOUN: An older, wealthy man who showers his young lover with gifts and financial compensation.

suggestive

(*suhg-JES-tiv*)

ADJECTIVE: Something that implies at vulgarity but is not explicit.

The young starlet knew exactly what she was doing when she chose to wear a dress with a SUGGESTIVE slit up the side to her meeting with the studio executives.

suitor

(*SOO-ter*)

NOUN: A male with romantic intentions toward a woman, specifically with the end result of marriage.

swinger

(*SWING-er*)

NOUN: Someone who lives a carefree sexual lifestyle, often marked by frequent exchanges of sexual partners (as in wife-swapping).

sybarite

(*SIB-uh-ryt*)

NOUN: One who devotes his or her life to the pursuit of pleasure; sensualist.

T

tantalize

(*TAN-ti-lyz*)

VERB: To tease or entice someone by letting him or her see something but not have it; tempt.

As seasoned burlesque performers, the sultry women know all the secrets to TANTALIZING the crowd without giving too much away.

tease

(*teez*)

NOUN: A person who teases others or intentionally arouses sexual feelings in another with no intention of satisfying the intimations.

temptation

(*temp-TAY-shuhn*)

NOUN: The act of being tempted or something that entices another to do something wrong, particularly in regard to sexual behavior.

temptress

(*TEMP-tris*)

NOUN: An alluring woman; femme fatale.

It is regarded as normal

to consecrate virginity in

general and to lust for its

destruction in particular.

—KARL KRAUS

thirst

(*thurst*)

VERB: To excessively desire something; as a noun the word refers to the need for a drink or liquid.

threesome

(*THREE-suhm*)

NOUN: A sexual activity in which three people take part; ménage à trois.

throe

(*throh*)

NOUN: An outburst of emotion or pain; can also be referred to in the plural.

tingle

(*TING-guhl*)

VERB: A sudden feeling of sensation such as vibration or stinging.

> *His body TINGLED with pleasure as his girlfriend slowly started kissing her way down his neck and chest.*

titillate

(*TIT-l-ayt*)

VERB: To stimulate or excite someone in a pleasurable way, often with a hint of sexuality; tantalize.

tomcat

(*TOM-kat*)

VERB OR NOUN: Engaging in a series of meaningless relationships for the purpose of having relations with as many women as possible; as a noun, *tomcat* refers to the man who does this.

toothsome

(*TOOTH-suhm*)

ADJECTIVE: Desirable or attractive; alluring.

transgression

(*trans-GRESH-uhn*)

NOUN: A crime or other wrongdoing that disobeys common ethics; indiscretion.

trollop

(*TROL-uhp*)

NOUN: A prostitute or other woman who engages in promiscuous behavior.

turn-off

(*turn-awf*)

NOUN: Something that causes a loss of libido in someone.

turn-on

(*turn-on*)

NOUN: Something that causes sexual arousal in a person.

Leslie is so infatuated with her new lover that even the faintest smell of his cologne is a major TURN-ON for her.

turpitude

(*TUR-pi-tood*)

NOUN: Extreme sinfulness.

two-time

(*TOO-tym*)

VERB: To carry on two sexual relationships at one time.

U

unbecoming

(*uhn-bi-KUHM-ing*)

ADJECTIVE: Improper behavior.

unchaste

(*uhn-CHAYST*)

ADJECTIVE: Impure or immoral.

uncontrollable

(*uhn-kuhn-TROH-luh-buhl*)

ADJECTIVE: Unable to be managed or controlled; unruly.

> *After spending the night flirting over drinks, the once strangers are now bedmates after rushing up to the hotel room in the throes of an UNCONTROLLABLE passion.*

uncurbed

(uhn-*KURBD*)

ADJECTIVE: Not restrained or controlled; unbridled.

undecorous

(uhn-*DEK-er-uhs*)

ADJECTIVE: Undignified or impropriety in behavior; indecent.

Society drives people crazy

with lust and

calls it advertising.

—John Lahr

unfaithful

(*uhn-FAYTH-fuhl*)

ADJECTIVE: Engaging in romantic affairs outside of a marriage or other committed relationship; adulterous.

unmoral

(*uhn-MAWR-uhl*)

ADJECTIVE: Neither moral or immoral; amoral.

unprincipled

(*uhn-PRIN-suh-puhld*)

ADJECTIVE: Lacking principles or morals; immoral.

unrestraint

(*uhn-ri-STRAYNT*)

NOUN: Characterized by a lack of restraint; debauchery.

unruly

(*uhn-ROO-lee*)

ADJECTIVE: Wild or out of control; disobedient.

unseemly

(*uhn-SEEM-lee*)

ADJECTIVE: Inappropriate or unbecoming; indecorous.

untoward

(*uhn-TAWRD*)

ADJECTIVE: Inappropriate or unbecoming; unseemly.

urge

(*urj*)

NOUN: A natural impulse or inclination; itch.

Finishing foreplay requires both partners to resist the URGE to skip the carnal appetizers and go straight to intercourse.

uteromania

(*yoo-ter-oh-MAY-nee-uh*)

NOUN: A female's uncontrollable desire for sex; nymphomania.

uxorious

(*uhk-SAWR-ee-uhs*)

ADJECTIVE: Excessively affectionate toward one's wife.

vagina

(*vuh-JY-nuh*)

NOUN: The tract that connects the uterus to the opening of the female's vulva.

vamp

(*vamp*)

NOUN: A woman who uses her feminine wiles to manipulate others.

> *Slinking around the bar with a sly but sexy smile on her face, the VAMP knew exactly what she was doing as she stole the attention of every male, partnered or not, in the place.*

venereal

(*vuh-NEER-ee-uhl*)

ADJECTIVE: Relating to sexual intercourse.

venery

(*VEN-uh-ree*)

NOUN: The search for or satisfaction of sexual delight.

Viagra

(*vy-AG-ruh*)

NOUN: A prescription drug used to treat impotence.

Love forgives the lover

even his lust.

—FRIEDRICH NIETZSCHE

vibrator

(*VY-bray-ter*)

NOUN: An electronic device that is used as a sexual aid.

vice

(*vys*)

NOUN: A bad habit or characteristic.

virgin

(*VUR-jin*)

NOUN: One who has never had sexual intercourse.

virginal

(*VUR-juh-nl*)

ADJECTIVE: Uncorrupted; characterized by someone who has never had sex.

virile

(*VIR-uhl*)

ADJECTIVE: Masculine or manly; strong or forceful.

virtuous

(*VUR-choo-uhs*)

ADJECTIVE: Righteous; virginal.

voluptuary

(*vuh-LUHP-choo-er-ee*)

NOUN: One who devotes his or her life to the pursuit of pleasure-seeking.

voluptuous

(*vuh-LUHP-choo-uhs*)

ADJECTIVE: Shapely and alluring; characterized by sensuality.

voyeur

(*vwah-YUR*)

NOUN: One who derives sexual excitement by (often secretly) observing others in the nude or engaged in sexual behavior; Peeping Tom.

Watching his neighbor through her bedroom window was an unbelievable turn-on for the VOYEUR.

vulgarity

(*vuhl-GAR-ih-tee*)

NOUN: Crudeness in behavior; tastelessness.

want

(*wont*)

VERB: To desire; long for.

wanton

(*WON-tn*)

ADJECTIVE: Uninhibited, particularly when it comes to sexuality; undisciplined.

weakness

(*WEEK-nis*)

NOUN: A lack of strength, sometimes as the result of a fierce fondness for something contradictory.

> *Dark hair and dark eyes were her WEAKNESS, and the charming man standing in front of her had both so falling for him was inevitable.*

well-endowed

(*wel-en-DOUD*)

ADJECTIVE: Having large genitals.

whore

(*hawr*)

NOUN: A woman who acts in a promiscuous manner; prostitute.

Sins become more subtle as

you grow older:

you commit sins of despair

rather than lust.

—Piers Paul Read

wife-swapping

(*WYF-swah-ping*)

NOUN: The consensual exchange of partners between two or more married or committed couples for sexual purposes.

winsome

(*WIN-suhm*)

ADJECTIVE: Something that is engaging or charming because of its innocence.

wolfish

(*WOOL-fish*)

ADJECTIVE: Having the characteristics of a wolf, including rapaciousness; *wolfish* can describe a man who is constantly trying to seduce women.

> *The WOLFISH man's slicked back hair and curled lip played into his wild persona as he moved about the party trying to seduce every women with whom he met eyes.*

womanize

(*WOOM-uh-nyz*)

VERB: When a man is constantly pursuing meaningless sexual relationships with women.

woo

(*woo*)

VERB: To pursue a woman, especially with the intention of marrying her; court.

worship

(*WUR-ship*)

VERB: To revere a person or thing as if it were a deity; adulation.

X and Y

x-rated

(*EKS-rayt-ted*)

ADJECTIVE: Describes graphic content that is not suitable for anyone under the age of seventeen because of extremely sexual or violent material.

XXX

(*eks-eks-eks*)

ADJECTIVE: The most graphic or explicit of pornographic content.

yearn

(*yurn*)

VERB: To long for or desire something greatly that some may consider a bit out of reach.

> *Separated by thousands of miles, the two young lovers YEARNED for the moment they would be back in each other's arms.*

Carnal lust rules where there

is no love of God.

—St. Augustine

Z

zeal

(*zeel*)

NOUN: Energetic enthusiasm; passion.

As he laid his hand on top of his wife's, whom he'd been married to for fifty years, a real ZEAL and passion overcame the two as if they were back in their twenties.

zest

(*zest*)

NOUN: Lively and spirited enjoyment.

Lust is to the other passions

what the nervous fluid is

to life; it supports them all,

lends strength to them

all . . . ambition, cruelty,

avarice, revenge, are all

founded on lust.

—Marquis de Sade

DAILY BENDER

Want Some More?

Hit up our humor blog, The Daily Bender, to get your fill of all things funny—be it subversive, odd, offbeat, or just plain mean. The Bender editors are there to get you through the day and on your way to happy hour. Whether we're linking to the latest video that made us laugh or calling out (or bullshit on) whatever's happening, we've got what you need for a good laugh.

If you like our book, you'll love our blog. (And if you hated it, "man up" and tell us why.) Visit The Daily Bender for a shot of humor that'll serve you until the bartender can.

Sign up for our newsletter at
www.adamsmedia.com/blog/humor
and download our Top Ten Maxims No Man Should Live Without.